LUDLOW'S SECRET GARDENS

Photographs by Sabina Rüber

text by Michael Dawson

with a foreword by

Cy Jones

Ampersand Books

on behalf of Friends of Ludlow Assembly Rooms

First published by Ampersand Books, Ludlow in 2004

Photographs © Sabina Rüber, 2004
Text © Michael Dawson, 2004

9 8 7 6 5 4 3 2 1

Ampersand Books
Ludlow
Shropshire SY8 1PP
SecretGardens@AmpersandBooks.co.uk

ISBN 0-905125-08-8

British Library CIP Data
A catalogue record for this book is available from the British Library

Printed and bound in China by Leo Paper Group: UK address, 94 High Street, Wallingford, OX10 0BW
Origination and setting by indetail : info@www.indetail.org

All proceeds from the sale of this publication will be donated by the Friends to Ludlow Assembly Rooms, South Shropshire's lively arts and community centre, which is a Registered Charity no.1010883

LUDLOW

River Corve

Ludlow Station

CORVE STREET

15

19 1

5

6

LINNEY

BULL RING

TOWER STREET

KING STREET

20

CASTLE

HIGH STREET

LINNEY

RAVEN LANE

BROAD STREET

10

11

DINHAM

8

12 9

BRAND LANE

BELL LANE

2 4

MILL STREET

OLD STREET

DINHAM
BRIDGE

13

River Teme

CAMP LANE

SILK MILL LANE

17

LUDFORD
BRIDGE

TEMESIDE

3

7

14

18

16

LUDLOW'S SECRET GARDENS

FOREWORD

Ludlow town centre is renowned for its fine architecture: the Norman castle, a magnificent parish church, medieval timber-framed buildings and elegant Georgian town houses. Many of its private gardens, however, hidden behind high walls or terraced facades, can rarely be seen.

Having lived and worked here for some years, I was often delighted to find friends' gardens for the first time and thought others might enjoy them too. In 1990 I put the idea to the test by arranging the first 'Secret Gardens of Ludlow' as a fund-raising event for the Friends of Ludlow Assembly Rooms - a voluntary group dedicated to supporting an arts and community centre then being planned for South Shropshire that opened soon after and is now firmly established. The June garden open-day proved an instant success and from that tentative start quickly became the Friends' most profitable regular event, attracting well over a thousand visitors annually and eagerly anticipated as a highlight of the Ludlow calendar.

Each year several new gardens are offered as well as some old favourites. Searching for fresh gardens was a delightful activity which I enjoyed for twelve years - the thrill of discovering a wonderful woodland garden behind an innocent wooden gate; the challenge of imagining how a garden might look in the summer when viewing it first in the bleak winter months; being invited to take a peek behind famous facades....perhaps discovering hidden treasures, unexpected glimpses of church or castle, or stunning horticultural gems. It was hugely rewarding.

Since 1990 over a hundred hosts have generously opened their gardens to us, some more than once, the record being six times! My entreaty that owners should do no more work than normal was largely ignored. A broken fence was mended; loose paving stones re-laid; ponds cleared; plants trimmed, tidied, moved - even occasionally borrowed from a neighbour to enhance a particular spot! None wished to present a less than perfect garden and we are grateful to each and every one of them.

In compiling the selection for this book (space sadly preventing us from including them all) we have, together with photographer Sabina Rüber, chosen a range of contrasting styles and sizes, each with its own special atmosphere, balancing horticultural interest with diversity of settings - sweeping lawns and topiary with tiny tub-filled courtyards; graceful statuary with pots of pansies, to give you a glorious pictorial flavour....a hint of the magic that lies within Ludlow's Secret Gardens.

Cy Jones.

Cy Jones

Secret Gardens organiser, 1990-2001

INTRODUCTION

I suppose most gardens hide secrets of one sort or another: the craftily disguised compost heap; the pile of builders' rubble transformed into an Alpine rockery; hopefully transplanted shrubs that failed to flourish - even occasionally (see garden no. 8) a buried Victorian mangle! But perhaps Ludlow's gardens are more secretive than most. Its centre is a textbook example of a medieval 'planted' (ie planned) town designed in a rigid grid pattern, no doubt for reasons of military expediency, along-side a mighty castle, the whole "...*wall'd quite round and pretty strong...*" according to William Stukeley writing in 1724.

Several garrisons of this sort were established on the Welsh border and elsewhere in England but few have survived intact during more recent urbanisation. Here, as some of the timber-framed buildings decayed they were replaced, during the town's second great period of prosperity, by fine Georgian mansions or public building that rarely infringed the earlier pattern. Thus, as Cy Jones has explained, many of the former burgage plots were transformed into a complex of trapped areas or gardens, often without rear entrance. Elsewhere, some newer houses were squeezed up to stretches of town wall, so are equally inaccessible except through front doors. These are not convenient arrangements for most modern householders but do provide those of us lucky enough to have call-ing-cards with many delightful surprises. It was a true inspiration to match our curiosity with the willingness of many owners to let us share these secret places.

This book is a celebration - indeed, might be deemed *mult-eye-celebratory* by some ebullient Americans. It is published to commemorate fifteen successful years of a scheme that brings pleas-ure to countless visitors from all over the Midlands - and further afield - at the same time raising substantial funds for a worthy cause. It extols the horticultural skills and unstinting enthusiasm of some of the garden-owners who have participated over the years and is offered as a small token of appreciation for their generous hospitality. And in particular, it celebrates the work of Sabina Rüber, a dedicated garden photographer whose knowledge, flair and seemingly unlimited patience have captured the spirit of these hidden spaces so ravishingly.

We have grouped pictures of the twenty featured gardens together, with a few words of introduction setting the scene for each. They are ordered roughly as a seasonal progression, though inevitably the majority were taken in the summer when things look their best. Owners and approximate loca-tions are indicated but not specific addresses, since none of the gardens are normally open to the public except on special occasions - the main one, of course, being organised each June by the Friends of Ludlow Assembly Rooms. So keep an eye open for future dates! In the meanwhile, regard this either as a lavish preview of pleasures to come - or a colourful souvenir of past visits.

Many helped make this book possible. Obviously, the owners whose participation was vital and was readily given. Jan Rose (who now Chairs the Friends) and Barbara Holcombe who have taken over the running of the Secret Gardens scheme gave invaluable advice and support, as did everyone on the Friends committee, particularly Pat Russell who, as Hon Teasurer, managed the finances. Merlin Unwin proved a fount of knowledge about the problems of publication. Paul Newman, with benign precision, turned it all into digits. And, of course, Megan who liaised, advised, calmed, and corrected (particularly my spelling and botanical gaffes) - for all this, and much more: my loving appreciation.

MD

Unlike the majority of gardens featured here, Lottie and Nick James's has been in the family for several generations.

In 1874 Lottie's great-grandmother Mary Green - who had recently been widowed - brought her four young children from Leinthall Starkes (near Wigmore) to live in Corve Street. Although some descendents moved away from Ludlow and many were born else-where, the quietly distinguished Georgian town house with its agree-ably informal rear garden has exerted a strong gravitational pull on her lineage ever since. Lottie's parents and family returned in the early '60s when she was nine; she then moved back in the '80s with young children of her own. The garden has graciously welcomed successive waves of boisterous youngsters and, of course, their numerous friends and pets.

Understandably perhaps, not a great deal has been altered over the years. Around the turn of the 19th Century an adjoining strip of land was acquired and the tall intervening wall has gradually been demol-shed, the reclaimed bricks used as bordering elsewhere. Steps and a central path across the upper lawn were moved, both to take advan-tage of this extra space and improve the croquet: the game has long been a family favourite and is still enthusiastically played. Recently a venerable yew tree near the house fell during a storm: a raised patio has been built in its place as an ideal eating-out spot in summer. And a decrepit greenhouse has been replaced by a modern one of similar size in the Victorian style.

About a third of the plot behind a hedge at the rear is devoted to vegetables. But although with Ludlow's excellent market there is hardly a need, the James's are proud to be almost self-supporting, propagating and nurturing a year-round crop. French-, runner- and broad-beans, lettuce, rocket, curly endives, parsnips, leeks and Swiss chard are staples as well as hard and soft fruit. Hens are also kept to fulfil breakfast requirements. Although this part of the garden is now somewhat overshadowed by an adjoining modern development, Lottie seems resigned to the change: "It blocks off our southern, win-er light between mid-September and mid-March so we're having to be more selective about what we plant. For instance, the broad-beans were a disaster in 2002 so we didn't bother with them last year - but that may have been due to other causes. We just don't know: we have to experiment." In fact one feels she may enjoy the challenge, since she readily confesses preferring: "....the fiddling-about-with-seeds-and-cuttings side of gardening to general mainte-nance." Hers seems a refreshingly non-interventionalist approach and perhaps others in the family will eventually follow with an equal

A view of the house across the lower lawn: roses and clematis frame the arch.

The new Hartley greenhouse with an inherited seat alongside and the raised croquet lawn behind.

Honesty glazed by the morning frost.

Frosted magnolia leaves.

In the cold, a dying hydrangea-head seems as if dusted with icing.

Swiss chard 'Bright Light': both leaves and stalks are eaten.

In the vegetable garden an urn, surrounded by a box hedge, forms a decorative centre-piece.

FIRMLY ESTABLISHED

2

Secret Gardens opening in 1991, 1992 and 1997.

Muriel Harvey is matriarch of the Bodenham clan - a family whose name has been inextricably linked with Ludlow for up to 150 years. Her great-great-grandfather came down from Clee Hill in the 1860s because he didn't like farming. He married the daughter of a local bonnet-maker and set up as a gentleman's outfitter, eventually moving into 600 year old premises near the Butter Cross - still occupied to this day by the family business, though now considerably expanded. "The line of succession has always been a bit bumpy," Muriel explains, "but fortunately each generation - almost by chance - has found someone willing to continue the tradition."

Her interest in gardening dates back to childhood. Her father returning from the First World War discovered that the firm - and its premises - were almost literally falling apart: although working elsewhere as an accountant he felt duty-bound to come back to Ludlow to rescue its fortunes. A house called 'Hendra' at Sandpits was acquired, surrounded by a large garden: Muriel (an only child) came to share his enthusiasm for tending it. Eventually, when she married and set up her own home (where she still lives) some of the plants and shrubs they had cultivated together found their way into the town centre garden on Dinham's southern slopes. One she remembers in particular - a sapling *Chamaecyparis* 'Wisselii' - was presented by her father as a moving-in gift: now huge, it boasts in season great trusses of pink coniferous flowers and is a magnet for song birds. Another was an Albéric Barbier rose that was growing wild over an outhouse at 'Hendra'. When a favoured Persian cat died, a bunch of the creamy-white flowers were laid on its grave. Amazingly, they involuntarily rooted and in time the new bush was lovingly transplanted to Dinham where it still flourishes gorgeously as the pet's memorial (when not threatened by knotweed!) over sixty years on.

Curiously enough, the house that she and her husband bought 36 years ago had previously been owned by a great uncle and aunt, though as a youngster she barely knew them. "It was they who created this garden at about the turn of the last century," Muriel says, "and basically it's still the same. They grew wonderful long-lasting things like white peonies and witch-hazel which go on

forever and are still enjoyed. Although improvements have gradually been made such as planting many more specimen trees, creating a small pond and adding an outdoor swimming pool, the main features haven't altered greatly over the years. Being on several levels is one of the joys: it's a garden you just have to accept as it is. I'm lucky to be in such a favoured spot where things do grow easily for me." Far from being complacent, though, she firmly believes in preserving what's good from the past and building on it for the future - which seems a sound maxim for business, life....and gardens!

Ornamental hares guard the garden front with wintering peonies and clematis behind.

Helleborus foetidus, prolific - and dramatic even in January.

From the terrace, the *Chamaecyparis* 'Wisselii' visible in the distance.

White hydrangeas beside the house, their dead-heads left to encourage future flowering.

Witch-hazel, probably planted over 100 years ago - blooms with exotic scent in December and lasts until February.

3

ON TEME'S EDGE

Secret Gardens opening in (1995), 1998, 2001 and 2003

For Megan Dawson who, along with her husband, first set eyes on their converted water-mill with its riverside garden in 1996, it was love at first sight. "I'm descended from four generations of millers," she explains, "tenants of a mill in the Ceiriog Valley, North Wales. So coming here was almost like returning home."

Nothing in her ancestry, however, prepared her for the garden, which incorporates an abandoned quarry, a river island plus the remnants of a complex scheme of terracing, dry-stone walling, a former tennis lawn, a bog garden (previously used as a swimming pool), steep steps and elevated hedge-flanked walkways - all of which, it is believed, were first landscaped in the early 1900s as part of the neighbouring garden. "It's an enchanting place," she says, "but quite a lot to take on - especially as neither of us were particularly keen or experienced gardeners." Her husband sometimes seems piscine rather than riparian - often claiming more pressing things to do - leaving much of the routine maintenance to her and an invaluable, knowledgeable Saturday morning helper, David Collier.

"For me, the last seven years have proved a rapid learning curve," Megan says. "It's by no means an easy garden to manage. To start with, it's on a steep north-facing bank - which means there are very few places that get good sun. Then we have a lot of big forest trees which create even more shade....plus much clearing of leaves in the Autumn. Naturally, it's very dry beneath the trees, especially on the slopes. And we have countless rabbits and moles - almost impossible to keep out from an adjoining copse...."

Despite such challenges and an occasionally elusive spouse, much has been achieved in reinstating the original scheme: both feel they are custodians rather than innovators. Paths have been excavated and re-surfaced; old wood removed or severely lopped; walling repaired; a circular walkway cut through dense undergrowth; much new infill planting, especially of shade-loving ferns, hostas and rampaging ivy as ground-cover. Where old trees have been lost at the river's edge (sometimes during flooding) more *Zantedeschia*, *Aconitum* and *Gunnera* have been spread along the margin whilst nearer the house herbaceous borders have been prudently thinned and re-stocked where appropriate.

Early morning frost on the lawn, once used for tennis and possibly for bowls.
Spring flowers, of which there are many varieties, spread widely along banks and terraces.

Erythronium 'Pagoda'

An upper path winds under an ancient yew - now connected to the lower levels forming a circular walk.

Euphorbia wulfenii which seeds prolifically - it glows with an
almost electric green, lighting up shady corners.

A pair of stone balls possibly
from the Butter Cross head steps to the lawn.

Riverside courtyard with *Euphorbia wulfenii* in the
foreground with winter pansies in the urn behind.

4

ARTFUL INFORMALITY

When Anne Lindsay moved here from her long-house home in Wales around two decades ago, she had a clear vision of what she wanted her garden to be - an even clearer one of what she wished to avoid: any hint of regimentation or formality. Her walled-in rear enclosure, little more than 100ft long by 40ft wide, lies on the southern slopes facing eastwards: when she arrived, it was nondescript and neglected. One of the few bonuses she found was a separate side access to the garden - something of a rarity in the centre of town.

With her daughter, Crystal (then living at home and "....an inspired gardener, though quite untrained...." according to her mother) they set about the conversion with military precision. Plans were drawn up, a ledger acquired to record all plantings (still scrupulously maintained, with 452 logged so far) and levelling began. As a student Anne studied at art school and the garden was to be an extension of her visual awareness: she wanted to make a place that would be tranquil, soft at the edges yet full of hidden pleasures. Despite its comparatively small scale, it was to be a sort of miniature wilderness; an ecological enclave, well before such a concept became fashionable.

Apart from a huge Bramley and two other apple trees that survive from the earlier garden everything else has been planted. Unusual trees and shrubs are carefully positioned, chosen as much for the beauty of their distinctive bark, foliage and berries as for blossom, though there is certainly no lack of seasonal colour. In amongst, bluebells, wild garlic, ferns and hostas grow in profusion, with occasional vivid splashes of intense colour provided by roses, peonies and a June flowering magnolia.

Stately white birches are a particular feature. "Maybe we planted a few too many at first - we went on our bicycles to buy them from a local farmer," Anne remembers. "Sadly, some eventually had to go to give other things breathing space. Other saplings were bought from the market...." she says, pointing to a twenty foot high tree. "From time to time the nurseryman who sold it to me comes to see how it's getting on!"

Few are lucky enough to watch such an ambitious scheme reach full maturity: what started as a vision has now become a veritable pocket-sized arboretum, exactly as intended: home to squirrels, frogs, butterflies, occasional hedgehog families and an abundance of birds - particularly a pet robin, so tame it now seems keen to pose for Anne's photographs.

The L-shaped seat was brought from Wales: overhanging, leaves of *Clerodendrum trichotomum fargesii*.

Crystal's stone, tile and gravel path flanked by box hedges, with a fine birch, *Betula jacquemontii* with its dazzlingly blanched trunk on the left.

Wild garlic *Allium ursinum*

A woodland bank of wild garlic growing amongst forget-me-nots.

A splendid *Viburnum plicatum* 'Mariesii' spreads in prostrate habit.

Viburnum head: the petals
cream the bracts pure white

One of the many unusual ferns:
Polystichum selifernum 'Divisilobum'.

A RE-INVENTED COTTAGE PLOT

When Jan and John Herbertson moved to Ludlow about six years ago, they found themselves confronting a wild, south facing strip of a garden: "A bit overgrown and with a lot of concrete," declares Jan, "but we saw it as a challenge and thought it would be fun to tackle."

Their house - a little out of the town centre - dates from the 1800s and was no doubt built as a semi-detached labourer's cottage, origially set amidst orchards and smallholdings. It now survives surrounded by Edwardian terraces and villas but still retains much of its original character.

John was a Royal Air Force pilot, so formerly the family led a somewhat peripatetic life. "We had four children so gardening in the early days of our marriage was just a matter of sprinkling a few marigold seeds and hoping for the best." says Jan. "As time went on, though, I started reading and visiting gardens and my interest was aroused. Then I volunteered to work at the Red House Museum garden in Christchurch, Dorset and became an enthusiast." Her husband concurs: "Jan provides all the inspiration; I do the digging and laying of bricks."

Their narrow plot now crams a great deal into a relatively small space, a riotous mixture of vegetables, fruit and flowers all happily competing for attention. Deliberately, there are very few straight lines or edges that are not luxuriously overgrown. Most of the plants are propagated in a small greenhouse or grown from seed, though some have been carefully transplanted from former homes - particularly a fig tree that survives from two gardens ago - it produced eleven eatable fruit last year! A few things are bought in: John particularly likes rescuing orphan plants from 50p boxes and nurturing them back to health. They were recently given an orchid that was pronounced as dead but after careful cossetting is showing promising signs of revival.

As a complete change of career, on leaving the Service, John took up blacksmithing and now runs a business in the town centre providing sculptural garden pieces (amongst other things) mostly on commission. He is an active member of the British Artists Blacksmiths Association and Ludlow Designer/Makers, with which he frequently exhibits. Naturally, examples of his skill pop up on his own patch, too - often in unexpected places. Jan also has an extra-mural interest in calligraphy (she's one of the Marches Scribes) and enjoys emulating Ian Hamilton Finlay by placing beautifully-lettered stones, as talismans, amongst the undergrowth.

Hardy geraniums, hollyhocks and roses are particular favourites and John has a liking for big prickly things - perhaps to compliment his wrought ironwork. Amongst the flowers grow garlic, raspberries, shallots and lettuces; behind glass, tomatoes and (John's speciality) hot chilli peppers.

The birdbath was inherited from a previous owner - re-positioned, it attracts constant visitors.

The much-travelled fig cutting against the shed, now happily established and bearing fruit.

One of John's 'rat tail' scrolls.

Jan's calligraphic stones bear the Italian greeting: "Hello Everybody!"

G.dalmaticum macrorrhizum

Geranium phaeum

Geranium 'Clarkei'

Gooseberries prosper amongst allium and chives.

6

LEDGED ON LINNEY

Secret Gardens opening 1999 and 2002

As one descends the steep steps to Rick and Val Alexander's garden, nestling below the remains of a town gate, it seems almost as though crampons will be needed to negotiate their beds and borders. Suddenly, though, one reaches a generous plateau from which their house and garden enjoy spectacular panoramic views over the water-meadows towards Long Mynd. In Anglo-Saxon times this was thought to have been a flax growing area ('lin' for linnen; 'hay' meaning mound) which may account for the rich top-soil, though Rick has a theory that this was tossed down the bank when the footings of the town walls above were being dug out in medieval times. Whatever the cause, the garden is now luxuriant, combining an ordered array of specimen trees, shrubs and eye-catching - often unusual - plants, particularly irises, which are something of a speciality.

They have lived here for almost ten years and have done much since to extend the house and improve the garden. Previously - for a time - Rick had switched careers to become a sheep farmer on Clee Hill where they had an acre of wind-swept garden and orchard to manage. Now they have a different set of challenges. Although smaller and more sheltered, their present, steeply-banked north-facing site tends to be dry. "Water quickly drains down, but so does the frost," complains Rick. "I'm afraid some of the trees have suffered." Because of the aspect, things tend to bloom a little later than in the centre of town.

Both Rick and Val are keen gardeners and share credit for the improvements which include a large conservatory, new levels, an extended lawn and a rear patio that boasts an impressive, multi-jetted fountain. Their next project is to reorganise the upper part, laid out as a series of terraces by a previous owner. "We plan to get rid of the precipitous steps and lay, instead, a winding path to give a gentler approach - one that can be negotiated with zimmer frames!" Rick jokes. However it eventually turns out, it's sure to be a trim solution since the Alexanders run a tight, well-mannered garden.

Irises 'Meadow Court' and 'Going my Way' (in the foreground) with *Allium aflatunense* behind.

Allium aflatunense

An elaborate fountain dominates the patio.

The new conservatory with the Parish Church towering behind.

Iris 'Going my Way'

7

PERFECTLY MATCHED

Our title refers to Neil and Val Aikens' quintessential English home and extensive riverside garden in Ludford which seem ideally complemented, in a way Miss Jekyll would have thoroughly approved. It might equally well refer to their owners who, when they moved here sixteen years ago were actually looking for a cottage! They fell in love with the garden - all three acres of it, as it then was - rather than the house: "That was much too big for us!" Val asserts but one can't imagine either house or grounds finding more sympathetic custodians.

Both house and garden are unusual. The timber-framed building (dated 1614 on its porch) is a copybook 17th century Shropshire structure perched above the Teme with captivating view of town and castle beyond. But it seems to have had a chequered history first as a merchant's house, then an inn before being divided in two. In about 1911 it then received a further comprehensive make-over by an itinerant Arts and Crafts architect - Basil Stallybrass - who stripped off accretions and attractively restored the interior. At the same time it is thought he probably laid out the garden using stone from an abandoned quarry to create a network of steps, riverside and terraced walks, raised borders, pathways and even a riverside grotto.

Several owners later, when the Aikens arrived, the structure of the Edwardian garden remained but for some time had been maintained rather than developed. Most would have been daunted by the challenge of reviving and improving it, especially as Neil worked elsewhere and still had five years before retirement. But not these two who slowly and systematically set about a comprehensive transformation. Shrubberies were grubbed up, hybrid tea roses replaced with ramblers or shrub roses, lawns laid, intruding walls demolished, overgrown trees near the house felled, paths re-surfaced....with new planting introduced everywhere. In time, a derelict outbuilding was restored as a revenue-generating holiday cottage, then sold as a dwelling together with a parcel of outlying land. That enabled work to be concentrated nearer the house where the aim has been to create a series of interlocking 'rooms' each with its own features and character. A splendid, inherited, yew hedge (ten feet high in places) fringes three sides of the property: on the river margin it delineates linking corridors; provides squints onto the river and grand walkways - all of monumental proportions.

A path to the arbour seat fringed by 'Winchester Cathedral' roses and *Nepeta* 'Six Hills Giant'.

A panoramic view of the town from an upper pathway, the castellated yew hedge in the middle distance.

'Rambling Rector' roses provide a perfect frame for the Haddonstone jardinière.

Inch thick quarry tiles, has been designated 'The Fernery'

A break in the massive yew hedge reveals a Java pumice sculpture.

THE VANISHED GARDEN

Secret Gardens opening in 1996 and 2002

When, a few years ago, Angela and David Edwards decided to move a little closer to the centre of town they found an ideal house - probably dating from the Regency period - right beside the Castle wall. The only problem was that it was rather larger than the two of them needed so they took the step which many in a similar position had trodden before: they decided to take in guests for bed and breakfast. The venture flourished and for over five years they found themselves with hardly a moment to themselves - especially during the lengthy tourist season.

Fortunately the town centre property - though spacious indoors - was walled around at the back, leaving only enough space for a modestly-sized courtyard. For the Edwards's this proved ideal since they had accumulated a mass of potted plants at their previous home. These, together with two well-established larger pots that were inherited from a previous owner (one containing a mimosa and the other, a spectacular clematis that spreads over a rear wall and balcony) were almost sufficient to create a virtually instant garden sanctuary that could be maintained with the minimum of effort. A few more were, of course, added to fill the gaps. As David says: "There would have been no time for digging or mowing. All that's needed with this sort of garden is an occasional bit of gentle forking-over and trowelling. In our enclosure we were even able to keep most of the slugs at bay....though we couldn't prevent a few attacking the hostas."

Despite surrounding walls - and the need to concentrate on shade-loving species - the east-facing area is something of a sun trap during summer months. Guests were invited to enjoy the leafy retreat, perhaps after their gastronomic excesses at famous local restaurants. Many found inspiration there, not only from the range of plants but also in the quirky manner in which they were displayed, using an old kitchen mangle (dug up from a former garden) and even a French metal cot (literally a 'flower bed'!) as features. There were even pieces of mock classical sculpture peeping from amongst the foliage - apparently left over from a Festival production of *Julius Caesar* some years ago.

Alas, since our photographs were taken, all these have migrated yet again: as Angela explains: "After all our recent exertions, we've decided to move a few miles out into the country, where we'll attempt to retire all over again" Though - with a larger garden to tend and plenty of voluntary commitments - Angela doubts very much whether they will find much time on their hands, even in tran-

From the french window: japonica on the wall hiding (or enhancing?) an old Ludlow mangle.

A 'Wonky Willow' duck hides under a patio table.

Hostas and hellebores growing in the French cot 'flower bed'.

Clematis and Rosa *Juabanville* climb the old wall.

Magnolia lilliflora 'Nigra' - in this sheltered spot it lasts well into the summer.

The magnolia in front of an old mail sorting-box,
now used as an effective garden-tidy.

Clematis and geraniums with ivy on the balcony; a reclaimed chimney pot
planted with Diascia; primulas against the cart-wheel hubs.

A REGENCY RETREAT

Secret Gardens openings in 1990, 1995, 1999 and 2001

Dick Stephens and his wife moved into their new home over thirty years ago and found the garden was neglected with piles of rubbish piled half way up some of the walls. As old Ludlovians, they had had their eyes on the place for some time: quite unlike other town centre properties it had been given a Cheltenham-style conversion in the 1820s with a leaded window hood, a charming ironwork balustrade on a wide balcony under which a generous loggia runs along the facade beneath - a wonderful adjunct to the sizable court-yard garden at the side.

In fact, the building is considerably older than first appears: originally double jettied and half timbered, it has received a number of makeovers in its 400 year history. Much of the timberwork was con-cealed, as was the custom during Georgian times when characteristic sash windows were inserted. Its garden front was then improved in Regency fashion before - later in the 19th Century - the main entrance was moved from the side so as to give access from the street. Now there are French windows along the courtyard which give the principal downstairs rooms a feeling of leading out into the garden and sharing the colourful and profuse planting.

Having excavated the accumulated detritus that was acquired on arrival, a York stone patio was created between what is now a kitchen/dining room and an old brick and stone-built coach house, presently serving as a garage. It has an elaborate Georgian dovecote on its gable: purely decorative, since it is eschewed by birds, much to the owner's relief. Low brick walls enclose the surrounding area providing a base for antique statuary and collected curiosities. There is a small water feature to give a welcome gurgle during the hot weather.

Other changes have mainly been to lawn and surrounds. The rectan-gular patch of grass they found has been extended and shaped to provide varied borders, now overflowing with specimen trees, shrubs and flowers. Although one baulks at the cliché, there seems no other description than 'a riot of colour' for this little sanctuary, slotted between surrounding properties like a jig-saw piece, a mere shout from the Castle's outer bailey.

The Regency facade with Wisteria climbing the columns, a *Cytisus battandieri* (Morocan broom) to the left and a row of scarlet potted geraniums guarding the balustrade like soldiers.

A fine display including foxgloves, hollyhocks and hardy geraniums.

Tall pink foxgloves match the proportions of the house.

Herbaceous profusion with a clematis 'Montana' against the far wall.

Rosa 'Moseii' was an early planting: brought from Mr Stephens' mother's house on Temeside in the 1970s.

GARDEN OF ILLUSIONS

Secret Gardens opening 2002

Barely a halberd's throw from the castle gatehouse is one of Ludlow's (Shropshire's?) most quirkily distinctive dwellings: reviled by some, overlooked by others yet cherished by many (especially its current owners) as a unique eccentricity. Designed as a small town house in the 1860s by a local - though rather obscure - architect Herbert Evans, it is a fantasy re-creation, mainly in high-quality polychrome brickwork, of a jettied Tudor building. The overall effect is of a tall, fancily-patterned jewellery casket sustained inside by a richly tiled hallway, finely carved oak staircase, elaborate door-cases, idiosyncratic fenestration and curious detailing.

When Jean and Paul Nicholls arrived nine years ago much of its charm had been obscured - even in places obliterated. With commendable zeal they set about retrieving its former distinction not only renovating or replacing but even furnishing it appropriately. But the dank back yard with its dilapidated wash-house proved something of a facer. Nothing daunted, they brought in a friendly landscape architect (Ian Dougal of Anthos Designs in London) who transformed this most improbable of sites, little larger than a cabbage patch, into a magical inner compartment. The wash-house was transformed into a garden room (now lit by an elegant glass cupola) alongside which a miniature iron and glass colonnade connects it to the house. A dimensional architectural metal frame set on concentric brick paving was constructed as a distinctive feature for climbing plants. Inset mirrors are used here and elsewhere to give the illusion of extra space and create myriad reflections.

"The garden is mostly Jean's inspiration." claims Paul. "Really, I prefer plants to have freedom so I have an allotment down near Dinham Bridge for my own pleasure. But granted the restrictions here, I think she has done wonders." Jean herself is more modest: "I wanted an off-beat effect that would match the house....rather like the gardens in Peter Greenway's films. But to be honest, I just didn't know enough about what to plant in such a restricted, shady spot. It wasn't until I asked plantswoman Angela Siminson to help that it began to work as I wanted."

Angela, who is also responsible for the garden at Mr Underhills feels that there are similarities between the two: the Nicholls' are great entertainers so their garden is constantly enjoyed by guests as part of the conviviality. "In such a confined space the problem is to provide things in flower through the year; we get round it by permutating the pots from time to time - some go to Paul's allotment and I take others that are out of season." It's a highly contrived arrangement: like the house itself, singular, whimsical and a little odd.

A general view from the Garden Room.

Architectural ironwork with hostas and Tiarella 'Iron Butterfly'. Clematis on the trellis, flanked by Laurus nobilis and bamboo Phyllostachys nigra.

Under the colonnade, an ingeniously angled mirror brings added light to the courtyard.

Lilium martagon blends happily with the *Clematis florida var. sieboldiana* on the trellis.

Trachelospermum jasminoides is trained against the walls of the garden room.

Betula utilis var. *jacquemontii* grows up into the cupola.

FLANKED BY ANCIENT WALLS

"When we came here seven years ago it was the house itself that really appealed to us but to find that the courtyard was already laid out so attractively was certainly an added bonus..." says Juliet Caithness, "....that and the fact that it also contains a workshop (site of two former cottages and a privy!) which I now use as a studio." She and her husband Dick already knew the town quite well and had determined to settle here on retirement. Neither was a particularly experienced gardener so an easily maintained - if somewhat confined - space suited them well. "The previous owners had brought in a professional designer who created levels and features," Dick explains, "and we liked the effect of the old, tile-capped surrounding walls contrasting with the garden's geometric design - plus the fact there's absolutely no mowing!"

None the less, they have made some significant changes. "Our predecessors planted several dwarf conifers which seemed to take up too much light and space, so we replaced all but one of them." Juliet continues. "We introduced more shrubs and flowers to bring colour throughout the year. We wanted to enjoy the changing seasons." Then a forgotten corner was tidied-up to make way for a pergola (now festooned with roses) to create an archway leading to the workshop - a great improvement, both agree.

One disappointment was the failure of a *Sorbus hupehensis* (Chinese rowan) intended as a central feature. Instead, the spot was paved with York stone and now makes an excellent slightly elevated patio for summer dinner parties. A small water-feature purls nearby, flanked by veined stones and smoothed pebbles, nicely complimenting the carvings displayed around - mostly Juliet's.

The new pergola lined with potted geraniums and overhung with 'Kiftsgate' roses.

Polly, their whippet, takes her ease alongside an emerging stone carving.

'Sweet Juliet' - "....how could we resist a rose with this name?".

One of Juliet's carved pieces: 'Eve'.

'Kiftsgate' rose

The eating-out area. Near the wooden bench, a sculpture by Peter Hibbert: 'Garden Nymph'.

12

FRUITFUL FORMALITY

Secret Gardens opening in 1999

For Julia and John Morrell, self-confessed amateur horticulturalists, their garden in Ludlow is the lesser of their responsibilities - they have another cottage in mid-Wales with grounds of some 30 acres (mainly vegetables and woodland) where according to John: "I do most of my hacking and bashing; chain-sawing and tractoring. We often return to Shropshire quite exhausted so it's a relief to have somewhere easier to maintain here."

Their fine, red-brick Georgian home was the Grammar School Headmaster's house for much of the last century: prior to that it was no doubt a merchant's dwelling with evidence of some sort of manu-factory on the gently-sloping burgage plot behind. When the School finally vacated it (and an adjacent building) to amalgamate into Ludlow College, a previous owner took the opportunity of removing some of the more dilapidated buildings at the rear. Subsequently the garden area was enlarged and completely re-styled in a slightly Italianate manner. Apparently it was a major undertaking with a crane brought alongside to lower huge pieces of stone to form patios, raised beds, paved walkways and a sizeable ornamental pool for water lilies and fish. Three descending walled 'rooms' were created, each with its own character and each enjoying spectacular views towards Whitecliffe.

"When we moved here about eight years ago, the planting at the top was fairly recent and all rather formal." Julia remembers. "Mostly it was unusual Australian shrubs and trees with an attractive fragrant magnolia. The lower garden has fine 100 year-old apple trees which of course we've kept. In fact, we like growing things we can eat so we've introduced many herbs and fruit trees to augment the existing planting. We're particularly pleased with a rather special espaliered apricot (bought at a school plant sale) which hasn't fruited yet but looks promising. We've also put in gooseberries, a fruiting mulberry, thornless blackberries plus red- and black-currants. All are now start-ing to crop - some even making sorbets for Christmas treats!"

Without a greenhouse the Morrell's propagate only a few things - in pots - mainly *Pelargonium* (geraniums) and herbs. But they are par-ticularly proud of their home-bred goldfish: a heron snatched those they originally had just after spawning, leaving only the tiddlers. Two generations later, with the pool now carefully netted for winter, its population exceeds forty.

Hardy geranium cultivar with *Astrantia major*
in a mixed herbaceous border, looking north
from the middle 'room'.

The apple tree decked with a splendid 'Rambling Rector' rose.

Magnificent blooms of the 'Rambling Rector' rose.

Against the far wall, espaliered apricot and greengage. The herb garden in the border includes several thymes, borrage, tarragon, curry plant and rue.

Climbing roses and clematis against an old brick wall.

Three of the 40 or more decorative inhabitants of the pool.

The ornamental pool with variegated *Fatsia* cascading over an adjoining wall.

13

DRINKS ON THE TERRACE ?

Secret Gardens opening 2002

Chris and Judy Bradley's terraced garden alongside Dinham Weir is probably easier to identify than others featured here - Mr Underhills is too well known to disguise. And, too, the garden is only semi-secret insofar as all who dine or stay at their highly-regarded 'restaurant with rooms' are privileged to share it.

We are fortunate to have attracted this energetic couple who sold their previous restaurant in Suffolk intending to re-locate elsewhere in East Anglia. But the deal fell through so they looked further afield - to Ludlow's great advantage. Arriving in late 1998, their first imperative was to prepare the premises for business but from the start the Bradleys had firm ideas for improving the garden. "We wanted it to be an outside lounge," says Judy, "but we needed instant results! So five years ago we called in a designer to do the hard landscaping. We asked him to create a series of outdoor 'rooms': you can appreciate them best from upstairs".

"A few of the plants we inherited and at first I filled the rest with bits and pieces bought from the market. But I soon realised that I needed some professional guidance so I called in an experienced plantswoman, Angela Siminson, for advice and practical help." For the last four years the two have worked in creative tandem - and the garden has flourished.

Angela found much of the soil terribly impoverished: loads of organic manure and compost were needed to improve it. Obviously, one of the basic requirements was for a coherent scheme with co-ordinated colour and variety throughout the seasons. Single-colour beds were jointly decided upon, some of which worked: others were deemed less successful.

Another intention was to include plants that would reveal their perfume to passers-by. And of course overall, the watery back-drop had to be taken into account. This has led to experimentation over the years: for instance on one occasion a predominance of white tulips, interspersed with pinks and purples, were chosen to fringe the river-edge - but somehow didn't seem quite right. Improvements are therefore continuous. "Every year we make changes," says Angela, "but they get smaller as we go along."

A mixed planting dominated by *Salvia officianalis*, the almost black rose 'The Prince' and lilac/pink 'Charles Rennie Macintosh' with Hosta 'Frances Williams' in the container.

'The Prince' Rose with *Salvia* and *Phygelius rectus* 'African Queen'.

A quiet eating-out area with 'Crown Princess Margareta' climbing Rose.

Alchemilla mollis and *Nepeta* 'Six Hills Giant' flank the walk-way.

Sculpture by Stuart Hill with *Astrantia major* 'Ruby Wedding',
Campanula latiloba 'Hidcote Amethyst' amongst *Heuchera micrantha*
'Palace Purple' in the foreground and 'Roseraie de l'Hay' behind.

Secret Gardens opening in 2003

Though retired, the Lloyd-Kitchens - Bill and Shirley - are a busy couple. Bill is an accomplished carpenter and joiner and seems to spend much time mending or making furniture for friends and relatives. Both are active members of the Parish Church congregation often providing voluntary support when needed. Shirley is involved with several other worthy causes. So when they moved into their present home in Ludford about eight years ago they needed a garden that would be pleasant to relax in, easy to maintain and capable of looking after itself during the times they would be preoccupied elsewhere.

Although one of a short terrace of seemingly identical cottages theirs is older than its neighbours and appears to have been re-orientated and comprehensively remodelled about two centuries ago. It has a typical, pocket-sized front garden: through its porched front door a central, quarry-tiled corridor provides the only access to the rear: a modest patch with a leafy north-eastwardly prospect that seemed on arrival full of potential. However, most of this area contained aviaries (the previous owner kept birds of prey) so these were quickly removed and a new lay-out planned from scratch. To contrast with the cottage garden at the front a more formal scheme was decided upon, and one that contained plenty of evergreens that would provide interest through the winter months. The lawn was largely re-laid; Bill undertook all the paving and stone-work (much in Victorian blue brick, rescued from a demolished stable); borders were dug and planted; containers positioned to show off box and ivy to best effect. Originally it had been intended to run the lawn somewhat nearer the house but an overhanging yew tree parched the grass so a small patio was created instead. A water feature was considered, then rejected: "After all, we're close enough to the Teme - we already enjoy the sound of water on the weir nearby."

A lot is already packed into the space, including Bill's workshop that might seem from photographs to be a standard kit shed but which actually he designed and built himself from carcass timber with a (reclaimed) clay tile roof. There seems little he can't turn his hand to. Indeed, both are now called in as consultants when other family-members seek help with their garden design.

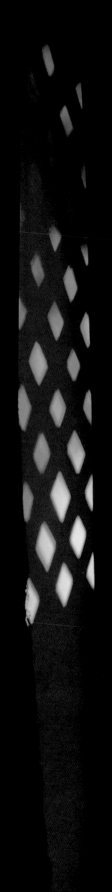

Max, the Lloyd-Kitchen's cat, off on an expedition.

From the patio: climbing hydrangea and a 'Madam Alfred Carrière' rose on the pergola.

The main (and only!) entrance surrounded by Hidcote lavender.

A glimpse through the front door to the more formal back garden.

A general view of the rear looking towards the house.
Again, lavender, box and ivy (on the iron obelisks)
dominate with Euonymus 'Albus' on the left.

Hidcote lavender - a Lloyd-Kitchen speciality.
Each summer it is gathered, tied in bundles and
sold in the Parish Church porch to raise funds.

15

LONG DOWN LINNEY

Secret Gardens openings in 1993, 1994, 1997, 1998, 2001, 2004

"It was the garden that sold us the house!" asserts Alison Taylor with her husband Julian's vigorous agreement. "We're gardeners - that's what we do with our time. It was finding somewhere near the town centre with a south facing, quarter-acre plot that decided us." Both were unconcerned that it was virtually derelict when they moved from Lancashire over twelve years ago - they had plenty of experience of coping having previously taken on a tumbledown farm near Chorley with similarly decrepit surrounds.

"It's much easier here," says Julian, "because the soil is good. We're not absolutely sure but assume that this was probably part of the original Carmelite priory garden. Although the 12th century ruins were finally cleared away over 200 years ago when we dig in winter we still find traces of old water courses. So most things grow well. Over the years we've put on tons of manure but can't say it's made an appreciable difference."

The garden was retrieved in stages without an overall plan - things were allowed to develop and evolve: the process is continuous. One thing was essential - to include generous space for vegetables. Although the Taylors do not quite achieve self-sufficiency, they are proud of their organic comestibles. Equally, they are keen on conservation so included a pool so as to attract newts and frogs. A recently-installed solar powered pump helps keep its water clear - but, to their disappointment, dragonfly larvae has tended to take over. "They eat the newts - they can be quite vicious. As a result we do have a lot of dragonflies!"

Julian is particularly interested in cultivating half-hardy *Salvia*, having about twenty varieties - some quite unusual - which have to be wintered in the greenhouse, also used for propagating and growing a variety of tomatoes. "In a garden this size you need to be quite ruthless with shrubs, either constantly pruning and trimming or taking cuttings before yanking them out and starting again. I tend to favour the latter."

Obviously both have their work cut out, especially as they also take responsibility for strimming and keeping tidy the nearby St Leonard's cemetery - now under the care of both the Church and Shropshire Wildlife Trust.

A general view of the garden: on the arbour grows Virginia creeper, variegated ivy and evergreen honeysuckle

A corner of the lawn with *Salvia darcyi* in the near border.

Tall red *Crocosimia* 'Lucifer' against the wall with yellow *Oenothera cinaeus* (evening primrose).

A teasel-like *Eryngium alpinum* 'Donard'.

'Gardeners' Delight' tomatoes. 'Alicante' and other varieties are also grown.

Virginia creeper hangs from the arbour behind which is a crowded border of salvias in many varieties.

A secluded pathway with pink and mauve Phlox.

16

A LUDFORD HIDEAWAY

Alan and Jean Turner's secret garden is even more concealed than most: hidden behind imposing gatehouse doors, through an archway then a further gate set in a tall leylandii hedge: the approach is almost like penetrating a Chinese puzzle! How surprising then to find that the formalities of an immaculately-ordered paved area near the house shades off into a woodland copse where grand old yews and conifers now blend with an extended lawn and newer planting.

Unlike many of the other gardens featured here the Turners were presented with a virtual *tabula rasa* when they arrived over 20 years ago. Having honeymooned in Ludlow before Alan's work took them all over Britain and abroad their return to Shropshire for retirement was almost by chance. The house they found seemed ideal. It had just been converted from outbuildings and stabling: its garden a mere patch of grass hastily laid to disguise builder's rubble. As both were reasonably enthusiastic gardeners they set about improving it with vigour.

Jean had some clear ideas: "Basically, I wanted something that would be easy to manage. Also, I was keen on a pool, though Alan took some persuasion! We planned the layout in stages: I remember putting out rows of baked bean tins so that we could visualize how it would all fit together. Originally the adjacent wooded area wasn't included but we negotiated to take over responsibility for it. During the conversion it had been used as a builder's tip, just a wilderness - so that took some clearing."

There were other problems as Alan explains: "What we hadn't realized at first was that there is a stone bed about 18 inches below the surface. That limited planting and of course makes for poor drainage. Although we are south facing the big trees of the woodland beyond bring more shade than we would wish; the roots sometimes intrude on the borders and their leaves during Autumn are a nuisance - especially in managing the fish pond. Those, and predatory herons from the river nearby. We originally tried to keep carp but they were all eaten!"

Despite such setbacks, they enjoy an enclave of almost cloister-like seclusion set against a backdrop of semi-wilderness.

The formal area with roses 'Cheshire Life' (red) and 'Just Joey' (apricot) in the border .

A fine 'Just Joey' bloom.

The fish pond which now contains Golden Orfe and Shubunkin with reeds and irises; mint is planted around for fragrance.

A woodland walk with agapanthus in the foreground and a reclaimed pig bench (originally used for slaughtering) now providing more restful service.

Superb water-lily nicknamed 'Delia' since it was given by a friend, Delia Compton.

17

AN INTRA MURAL GARDEN

Secret Gardens openings in 1991, 1992, 1993 and 2002

There can be few town houses that boast such venerable or extensive boundary walls as the Cundall's. Their garden stretches along the top of the old town wall including the last remaining bastion (look-out tower) originally guarding Ludlow's southern approaches. For about 200 yards the garden is in the form of a corniche, backed on its northern edge by a much-restored high brick retaining wall built as a series of elegant blind arches. In the summer it is a sun trap blessed with panoramic views of the Teme winding below and the precipitous tree-covered Whitcliffe escarpment on the opposite bank.

The garden was smaller when Richard and Alison arrived in 1988 and not so well cared for. Indeed there seemed to have been few substantial changes since Georgian or early Victorian times when various specimen trees such as larches and Scotch pines were planted, some inappropriately close to the walls - which themselves were in poor repair, often dangerously so. Richard was under no illusion as to the problems they were inheriting: "We encountered major structural problems both with the house and in the garden. Naturally, we had to tackle the building first to bring it to modern standards. But our main headache with the garden was to reach a compromise between those who advised that the trees must be retained at all costs and others who required us to conserve the walls which are of course a part of the town's heritage."

For Alison, the solution was clear: "I tend to the view that trees are replaceable but old edifices aren't - once they are allowed to fall, they've gone for ever. So we felt bound to take down some of the old trees especially where the roots were destroying stonework. We've planted many more than we've chopped down - mostly fruit - but always clear of the walls. As time has gone on we have been able to modify the layout and add to the garden but there's never been a grand design - we prefer to let things evolve gradually. For instance we removed a path that ran along the upper brick wall so as to create a wider herbaceous border. I considered getting a landscape designer to create new pathways but I've now worked out a scheme of my own....that's probably our next big project."

An earlier achievement was the creation of a knot garden the plan for which was inspired by one at the Museum of Garden History. Laid out in 1999, it sorely tested Alison's geometry but is now maturing well and, set below the bastion from which the pattern can best be appreciated, shows no lack of mathematical skill. In amongst the maze-like miniature box hedge planting, metal sculptures of a cockerel and two pullets scratch, larger than life - they are by local craftsman Finn Kay whose work in differing styles can be found elsewhere around the garden. "We wanted to introduce a few hard edges and changes of texture," explains Richard, "too much greenery and shrubbery can sometimes seem a bit boring."

The patio with urns rescued from a neighbouring garden planted with ivy and geraniums.

White Agapanthus cultivar

A vista of the house with a modern sun-dial and antique stone lion set on the lawn around which snaking pathways are planned for the future.

The knot garden with metal hens: the ancient bastion is behind.

8 WALL'D QUITE ROUND

Secret Gardens opening in 1998

William Stukeley's comment on Ludlow (quoted in the introduction) might equally describe many of the town's houses and gardens - but none more aptly than Frieda and Derek Williams's which occupies - alongside neighbours - what was an extensive walled kitchen garden. Originally this was the domain of famed head gardener W.A.(Bill) Bengree whose legendary topsoil was apparently spirited away when the two single-storied homes were built - more than a decade ago - over vegetable plots he had lovingly fed and nurtured. A carved stone is set in the wall outside the enclosure to commemorate him: he died, aged 73, in 1986.

The Williams were not the first owners of their home: its builder occupied it for a while and laid out the garden. "Neither of us are particularly knowledgeable gardeners," explains Frieda, "and we were glad to find somewhere relatively easy to manage. During the past ten years we have extended the flower beds and moved some of the shrubs to more suitable places. We love the yew trees at the top of the garden but they stole all the moisture from the row of nine speciality rhododendrons that had been planted beneath them, so they failed to flourish. We are gradually replacing them with choisya, berberis and plants like sweet woodruff that tolerate dry and shady conditions."

What has evolved is a garden with three distinct parts, says Derek: "There's the lawn area which is shaded at the top; the courtyard con- tained between the wings of the house and a separate walled area around the back. At the top of the lawn is an old well that *might* be '....the far-famed healing well at St Julian....' mentioned in The History and Antiquities of Ludlow (1822). It appears from old maps to be in the right position.

Poised over one corner of the garden are two large metal storks take- ing startled flight: a specially-commissioned work by Christy Bowdler, ornamental blacksmith from Cleobury North. Frieda and Derek knew they wanted something dramatic here so worked closely with the designer to realize a spectacular eye-catcher. Elsewhere - in the walled area - a sizable metal mobile sculpture by Paul Margetts (based at Belbroughton) revolves intriguingly in the wind, its reflec- tion caught in a cleverly positioned *trompe-l'œil* wall feature.

Christy Bowdler's metal storks lift off amidst hebes and euphorbia with sugar cane growing elegantly alongside

Another view of the storks with a low acer (Japanese maple) turning red in the foreground.

Autumn-tinged euphorbia with reeds forming the background.

A few remaining florets of *Hydrangea petiolaris* before the Autumn fall.

The climbing hydrangea cascading over the courtyard pool.

Camellia bushes frame an ornamental trellis in the walled area.
A centrally mounted mirror giving a corridor-like impression.

Japanese anemone
'Honorine Jobert'

PUBLISHERS' PLEASANCE

Secret Gardens openings in 1994, 1995 and 2001

Karen and Merlin Unwin, partners in an expanding firm of specialist publishers, relocated from London (on an impulse, they maintain) and now - enviably - live in a congenial Georgian town house right next to their business premises. How's that for a shrewd move?

Before they arrived well over a decade ago their experience of gardening had been confined to metropolitan patches: here they acquired a double burgage plot that required serious tackling. Merlin (who's a committee member of the Ludlow Horticultural Society) had firm ideas: "We found the garden well-tended but not really to our taste: mostly lawn and little bedding areas - a bit municipal. Then at the end there was a massive fruit cage (it had once supplied soft fruit for the Feathers Hotel when its owners lived here) but it had fallen into disrepair so we decided to scrap it. I drew a map of the intended lay-out: decided to introduce a little formality. First we set a herring-bone brick path right across the lawn leading up to a brick semi-circle and dividing yew hedge. Behind this we later constructed a round, stone-surfaced sunken area. Beyond, where the fruit cage had been, we made a flower bed. Near the house we retained the lawn as a play area for our four young children. More recently, we've built a pergola and, last year, a wattle summer-house - it presently looks a bit raw so we've nicknamed it 'The Bus Shelter'! But it should weather nicely in time."

Effectively this has divided the garden into four contrasting spaces but much remains to be consolidated. Yew hedges are being planted which will eventually be trained into archways so as to make the compartments even more discrete. Even topiary is being considered along the dividing yew hedge. Much planting around the sunken area is creating an aromatic secret enclave and shrubs are being propagated (with varying degrees of success) to re-stock the many herbaceous borders. Merlin sees it as a long term project: "The wonderful thing is that we're both happy here. Ludlow's a marvellous place where we plan to stay. I've always believed that gardens need time to develop a distinctive character. Ours is now perhaps two thirds of the way towards completion of the original scheme though we'll no doubt continue to make modifications. It's good to think of gardens as an investment and to look forward to enjoying the maturing benefits...."

The Unwins designed their summer house using hazelwood wattle panelling by Adrian Thorius whose workshop is near Clun.

A shady corner overhung with *Cotoneaster exburiensis*. The lion's head is *faux antique* and is eventually destined to peer out of a mature yew hedge.

Berberis thunbergii providing beautiful autumn colour.

Lovely ray-florets of *Hydrangea villosa* turning pink with age.

ON HALLOWED GROUND

Secret Gardens openings in 1990, 1992 and 2001

Long before it became fashionable to convert redundant churches for domestic purposes, Betty and Paul Smith acquired the abandoned Congregational chapel (which surely must have been Ludlow's most well-concealed places of worship, proudly dated 1830 on its pediment) then set about turning its shell into a gracious, tucked-away home. They came to Shropshire almost half a century ago to set up an antique business (yet still light-heartedly accept themselves as mere incomers!) living above the Church Street shop for several years. Then in 1969 they bought the chapel and set about its conversion moving in about five years later. The tiny surrounding burial ground posed unusual problems though, as a free church site the land was not consecrated. None the less, each grave was plotted and permission asked of surviving relatives for changes to be made. None objected so memorial stones were moved to the edge or used for paving.

Surrounded on all sides by walls it was not the easiest space in which to create a garden. At the front, it receives little or no sun especially in winter. On the remaining open side it is a sun trap which can bake things in hot weather. In the early years, they benefited from the friendly advice of David Wright who had moved here from Cambridge where he had worked for the Botanical Gardens: many carefully selected trees and shrubs were planted to take account of the unusual conditions. Alas, the severe winter of 1982 killed off almost everything - so the Smiths had to start again, virtually from scratch.

"Since then, we've mostly worked on the Topsy Principle," says Betty, "...putting things in to see if they will take; moving them if they don't seem happy; fiddling around to get the best results. It was poor ground when we came - not intended for growing. So we had to build raised borders and put in tons of soil. But we found herbaceous plants were no good at all in such a confined space - they just grew tall and leggy. So we concentrate mainly on more specimen trees and shrubs (for instance, we have a wonderful *Corylopsis pauciflora* in the front (experts say they've never seen one as big in a private garden) with lots of bulbous things for the spring - specie crocuses and small daffodils (I don't like the big floppy ones), chinodoxia, scilla, and ferns, of course....lots of ferns. Shropshire is Fern County after all"

view from the entrance gate with akebia in the foreground and behind two elegant *Cypress chamaecyparis* columnaris matching the height of the building. In their early days, these were netted to encourage slender growth.

An individual, delicate *Stellata* bloom.

The side garden in spring with dog-tooth violets in the foreground and a magnificent early *Magnolia stellata* flowering on the left.

Paul re-modelled 'The Orangery' from a dilapidated Sunday School. Ironically there are no oranges - a lemon tree flowers but refuses to fruit!

A hosta dying back for winter: the leaves can be particularly parchment-like and luminous in their final days.

SABINA RÜBER was born in Zürich but has lived in the UK
for nearly 20 years. She is married with a young son and
lives near Ludlow in North Herefordshire. After initial
training at the Zürich School of Art, she obtained a Higher
National Diploma in Documentary Photography at Gwent
College, followed by MA (Photography) at the Royal
College of Art in London. She has been a visiting lecturer
at Derby and Sunderland universities and has undertaken
commercial commissions in Britain, Switzerland, and
Spain. Her work appears in many leading gardening and
life-style magazines.

MICHAEL DAWSON is a fine arts graduate who has
worked as an industrial designer, art teacher, youth leader,
head of an adult education centre and as director of both
Greater London and Yorkshire Arts Associations. He and
his wife retired to Ludlow seven years ago where they now
deal in children's books - which he also repairs, researches
and writes about.

Front Cover photograph from garden no.12 : Frontispiece from garden no.3 : Back cover from garden no.7